I0157410

The Three Things the Rest of Us Should Know about ZEN TRAINING

Dennis E. Bradford, Ph.D.

Publisher's Notes

ISBN 978-0-9882623-7-9

completeness of the information in this book. The author and publisher shall in no event be held liable for any loss or other damages including, but not limited to, special, incidental, or consequential damages.

Any and all product names referenced within this book are the trademarks of their respective owners. None of those owners has sponsored, authorized, endorsed, or approved of this book. Always read all information provided by the manufacturers' product labels before using any product. The author and publisher are not responsible for claims made by manufacturers.

The author only recommends products that he has personally read or used and found useful. Please do your own due diligence before purchasing anything.

This book is for your own personal use only.

Any perceived slight of any individual or organization is purely unintentional.

Printed in the United States of America.

Also by the Same Author

The Concept of Existence
The Fundamental Ideas
Mastery in 7 Steps
How to Survive College Emotionally
A Dark Time
Personal Transformation
The Meditative Approach to Philosophy
How to Eat Less – Easily!
Compulsive Overeating Help
How to Stop Emotional Eating
How to Become Happily Published
Belly Fat Blast with Anna Wright
Getting Things Done
Weight Lifting
Emotional Eating
Love and Respect
12 Publicity Mistakes that Keep Marketers Poor
It's Not Just About the Money!
40 Top Marketing Mistakes

Contents

1: Introduction

Freud, for one, understood **the problem**. Near the beginning of <u>Civilization and Its Discontents</u>, he writes: "Life, as we find it, is too hard for us; it brings us too many pains, disappointments and impossible tasks. In order to bear it we cannot dispense with palliative measures."[1] We need something to help us get through our days.

Freud thinks that "perhaps" there are three kinds of such measures: "powerful deflections, which cause us to make light of our misery; substitutive satisfactions, which diminish it; and intoxicating substances, which make us insensitive to it."[2] Unfortunately, none of these work well. For Freud, the problem is irremediable.

Fortunately, Freud was wrong. **Meditation can cure the problem.**

Furthermore, he was wrong in an interesting way, which is always the mark of a good thinker. Since his view of what it was to be a human being was incorrect and since his thinking about how to treat the problem relied upon his theory of human nature, he had no chance to locate the cure. Axiological theories, theories about value, always depend upon underlying theories of human nature.[3]

The claim that meditation works critically depends upon the truth of a certain view about human nature. Since what is most distinctive about human animals is our minds, it's not surprising that the claim that meditation works depends upon the truth of a certain view about how our minds work. This view is clarified in what follows.

There are many kinds of meditation. Although the one that is of primary interest here is Zen training, much of what follows is applicable with minor adjustments to other kinds of meditation or body practices.

What would someone for whom Zen training is alien want to understand about it? Three things:

(1) **What is its purpose?**
(2) **How does it work?**
(3) **Is it for me?**

2: Meditation

All meditation is based on the idea that states of mind are what really count. Heaven and hell are not places; rather, they are states of mind. **Dissatisfaction (discontent, misery, suffering, <u>dukkha</u>, off-centeredness) is our default condition**. If we do nothing, we'll continue to be dissatisfied until we die. Our lives will continue to be hellish. Why? It's because we'll simply remain enslaved by our untrained (undisciplined, impure, over-active) minds.

If we really want to live well, however, it is possible. Freedom is our birthright. Some humans have understood this at least since the Axial Age 2500 years ago. The real problem is not theoretical.

It's the practical problem that we must claim our birthright. Initially, it's like having an inheritance without realizing that we have it. It's already ours, but we won't get it until we claim it, and we cannot claim it until we realize that we have it coming.

Furthermore, once we realize that we need to claim it, we may not understand how to claim it. Claiming it requires training the mind, which is very difficult. Nobody can train another's mind, and **nobody lives well with an untrained mind.**

The training required is very simple. All meditation comes down to is noticing when the mind is being undisciplined and returning its focus to the practice. Noticing and returning, noticing and returning-- thousands of times![4] With perseverance, instead of being incessantly controlled by the mind, we become able to control it.

Meditation is the cure for the dis-ease that afflicts us all. There's nothing wrong with the mind itself; rather, what's wrong is our persistent misuse of it. All that is required for living well is that we stop misusing our most important ability, which is our ability to control our focus. It's possible for you to prove that for yourself.

We misuse the mind as long as we continue to let it do whatever it wants. What it wants to do is to keep conceptualizing *incessantly*. Let's ensure that we understand conceptualizing and then discuss this.

To have a mind is simply to be aware or conscious. Awareness or consciousness is always about some object or other. Some of those objects are concepts and the judgments we make using concepts.

Concepts are principles of classification, typically qualities (commonalities) or sets of qualities. To conceptualize is to judge that some object is a member of some kind (sort, group, category) or other. I might judge, for example, that this is a table or that that shirt is red. So judgments are conceptualizations, which are just classifications (separations, divisions, sortings, bifurcations) of objects.

To understand something correctly is to make a true judgment about it, whereas to misunderstand is to make a false judgment.

There's nothing at all wrong with conceptualizing itself. In fact, it's required for survival. Obviously, it's better to be good at conceptualizing, to have good understanding, than otherwise.

There is, however, everything wrong with being in thrall to the tyranny of *incessant* conceptualization. Instead of using the mind to assist us to live better, we are constantly letting our great capacity run amuck. We cannot ever be free until we put an end to that tyranny. **Living well requires using the mind well, and**

using it well requires training (disciplining, purifying, stilling) it.

Breathing is natural and critical. A spiritual practice (meditation, Zen training, yoga) is a practice based on awareness of breathing. It's a body practice. Since breathing occurs in the present moment, a spiritual practice is based on awareness of the present moment. It has no more to do with anything religious or supernatural than it has to do with the past or the future.

There's nothing theoretical (conceptual, intellectual) about meditation. It's not a matter of explaining or understanding anything. It's a matter of doing something, namely, **persistently practicing directing the mind** so that its focus is on where one wants it instead of elsewhere.

It's similar to training an animal. It's not a matter of explaining something to the animal to get it to understand something so that it will voluntarily comply. Imagine trying to teach a dog the germ theory of disease so that it will voluntarily defecate outside one's home! There's nothing theoretical about training an animal. Instead, it's a matter of persistently getting the animal to do what one wants it to do instead of allowing it to do whatever it wants to do.

However, you may deny this. You may not realize that you are unable to control your mind. Until you do, you will remain unable even to begin to appreciate the value of spiritual training.

You may think yourself able to concentrate whenever you want. For example, pick some object and focus on it for half a minute or a minute. Go ahead. Pick an object in your visual field, perhaps the corner of a table. Take a breath and lock it in. Focus on that corner for thirty seconds. No problem, right?

Actually, there is. If you take the same test for long enough to require you to breathe, you'll likely find it impossible. If you have any doubt at all about this, please prove it to yourself. It won't take long: simply take the same test only make it five minutes long. Just focus on the object you have selected for five minutes. Simple, right? Yes, it's a very simple test.

Easy? Well, no. Try it. Don't think about the object—or about anything else. Don't make any judgments whatsoever. Don't conceptualize at all. Just stare. Just focus on it with all your might. Pay full attention to it— and to nothing else—for five minutes.

If you are able to do that, you may not need meditation. However, without having already had some kind of spiritual training, it is impossible to pass that simple test. Within a couple of minutes, some extraneous judgment will occur to you. You'll think about some food that would taste good or an errand that you forgot to run or the weather for the event tomorrow or something about a television program or the causes of the sound you just heard—you'll make some judgment or other.

Failure doesn't mean that you are abnormal. It simply means that you are unable to control your mind for even five minutes.

This is an extremely important realization. Please appreciate it.

Ask yourself this follow-up question: "Since I am unable to control my mind for five minutes, is there any further reason to wonder why I am dissatisfied with (aspects of) my life?"

Without paying attention to it, there's no way any experience could be really rewarding. Genuine satisfaction requires full attention.

To meditate is to train yourself how to pay attention well. It's to train yourself how not to suffer from a split between where your attention is and the present moment (for example, what you are doing). To paraphrase a contemporary Zen master, practicing meditation is a clever way to enjoy life.[5] Meditation, in other words, is not an escape from life: it's a way to experience life more deeply. Without giving it our full attention, the present moment could not possibly be richly rewarding.

The present moment is the only moment we have to live.

Zen training is spiritual training, meditation. Its purpose is to enable us to live better by enabling us to live more fully in the present moment. It is able to do that because **zen training cures the disease of the mind, inattentiveness, which prevents us from living well.**

3: The Benefits of Meditation

There are many benefits of a daily meditation practice. Some benefits are more important to some people than other benefits. Let's agree to classify the most important benefits of Zen training as "primary" and to classify all the other benefits as "secondary." (This does not mean that the so-called secondary benefits are less important to a particular practitioner [trainee, student] than either of the so-called primary ones.)

In no particular order, these are the **secondary benefits** of Zen training:

Improved concentration
Decreased emotional instability
Clearer conceptualization
Greater independence
Decreased emotional eating and similar detrimental
     behaviors
Decreased stress
Decreased tensions, anxiety, and nervousness
Increased creativity and spontaneity
Improved work performance
Lowered blood pressure and blood lipid levels
Increased acceptance of oneself
Increased acceptance of others
Increased ability to overcome self-damaging behaviors like
     addictions
Greater intimacy with loved ones
Others become more attracted to the practitioner

These are the two **primary benefits**:

1. The practitioner may be able to empty the mind completely of all judgments, which is known as "awakening" (the experience of no-self, satori, kensho).[6]

2. The practitioner may be able to infuse the insight from awakening throughout all activities, which is known as "enlightenment."

The second primary benefit cannot occur without the first. Since a practitioner who continues Zen training after awakening will experience more profound enlightenment, enlightenment comes in degrees. With continued training, one will be more enlightened ten years after a breakthrough awakening than after ten days. (The idea of a sage who becomes fully enlightened is more an ideal than a reality.)

Spontaneous breakthroughs, in other words, ones that do not come as a result of Zen training or another deliberative body practice, do occur. Since freedom is our natural condition, this is hardly surprising. In fact, it would be surprising if there were never any spontaneous breakthroughs. However, since there's no way to expand or deepen them without training, they have no lasting impact on the quality of someone's life. They are interesting experiences but so isolated that their importance is negligible.

If one's training is sufficiently intense and persistent, the patriarchs assure us that awakening will occur. A chief reason why training to achieve the primary benefits is so difficult is that, short of awakening, there is no way to determine how well one's training is going. It's like a man traveling in a fog who has no idea how close its lifting is. Alternatively, it's like undertaking the task of hiking 100 miles up a mountain and being told that there won't be any indications of how far one has hiked until the 50 mile point.

Awakening is not the real purpose of Zen training; it is, however, the first of the two important goals. **Enlightenment, which is using awakening to live well, is the real purpose of Zen training.**

4: The Buddha's Ideas

Meditation seems to have originated in India prior to historical records. After studying with some Hindu teachers, the historical Buddha developed a distinctive kind of meditation that eventually became popular in China, where it was influenced by Taoism, and later in Korea and Japan.

'Zen' is simply the Japanese word that translates the Chinese word 'ch'an.' 'Ch'an' is just a transliteration of the Sanskrit word 'dhyana.' 'Son' is the corresponding word in Korean. All of them mean 'meditation' (and none of them were words that the historical Buddha actually used[7]). From here on then, let's use 'meditation' and 'zen training' interchangeably.

The Buddha never wrote any books, but some of what he said was preserved by his disciples as best they could and eventually written down. Contemporary Zen masters trace their lineage back to the Buddha, who was unquestionably one of the greatest spiritual geniuses and most important human beings who ever lived.[8]

It's important to separate Zen training from religious accretions as well as from other forms of meditation. Zen Buddhism is not a religion. It's a practice, **a way of living**. There's nothing supernatural about it. It has no creed. Individual practitioners are not subject to authority, but instead they are encouraged to uncover the truth for themselves by their own efforts. It is neither speculative nor theoretical. It is independent of book learning and even of tradition.[9]

The only belief (confidence, faith) required to practice Zen training is the belief that it might be beneficial. This is no different in principle from the belief needed to begin, say, to practice the piano or to learn how to skate. There'd be no reason to begin any practice unless one thought that one is capable of it and that one might benefit from mastering it. As one benefits from the practice, the need for belief diminishes. Since they have actually discovered its benefits, masters of any practice need no belief in it. Belief evaporates with success.

The Buddha is quite clear that, although the training is difficult, it is worth it. He says that a mind being trained in meditation "thrashes about in agony" like a fish hooked and left on the sand.[10] The mind resists discipline, but disciplining it brings benefits essential to living well. Let's here consider Zen training by looking briefly at what he actually said about it.

"Hard it is to train the mind, which goes where it likes and does what it wants. But a trained mind brings health and happiness . . . They are wise whose thoughts are steady and minds serene, unaffected by good and bad. They are awake and free from fear . . . Wake up! Don't be lazy."[11] **Training the mind means disciplining it in order to live better.** It means going beyond our egocentric evaluations, including—and especially—our egocentric preferences concerning what is good and bad. It results in practitioners becoming healthier and happier with balanced minds. Yes the training is difficult, but failing to train the mind, which is the only alternative, is much worse.

To wake up is to become "free of all conditioning."[12] To wake up is to let go of selfish attachments: "Don't get selfishly attached to anything, for trying to hold on to it will bring you pain. When you have neither likes nor dislikes, you will be free. / Selfish attachment brings suffering . . . Selfish bonds cause grief . . . never try to possess people and things."[13] The problems of living are caused by our selfish attachments to which we are addicted. To let them go is to wake up to freedom.

To wake up is to become wise. "The wise are disciplined in body, speech, and mind."[14] Meditation is the way to wake up. "Meditation brings wisdom; lack of meditation leaves ignorance. . . **There can be** no meditation for those who are not wise, and **no wisdom for those who do not meditate**."[15]

Acting morally comes from being wise. "Those who meditate and keep their senses under control never fail to do what ought to be done, and never do what ought not to be done. Their suffering will come to an end."[16] This moral ideal is the ideal of living well. "Best among men is one with a well-trained mind. . . best of all is to be an illumined sage."[17]

So living well comes from breaking the natural bonds to what we like by using meditation to overcome selfish attachments. "All human beings are subject to attachment and thirst for pleasure. . . Overcome this thirst and be free."[18] He knows this because he has experienced it. "I have conquered myself and live in purity. . . I have left everything behind, and live in freedom."[19]

We can do the same thing by training ourselves to serve others. Someone lives well who "meditates deeply, is at peace with himself, and lives in joy . . . [w]ith friendship toward all."[20] So meditate! "Raise yourself by your own efforts . . . be your own critic. . .Be your own master and protector."[21]

The key is to "[g]o beyond all likes and dislikes" by using meditation to train the "mind to be still" and to reach "the supreme goal of life."[22] **The mind is like a tool or resource to be used**: "As irrigators lead water where they want, as archers make their arrows straight, as carpenters carve wood, the wise shape their minds."[23]

The Three Things the Rest of Us Should Know about ZEN TRAINING

The quality of our lives is determined by how we use our minds. "Our life is shaped by our mind; we become what we think."[24] If we take control of our minds, we will live freely and well. Don't settle for a good life when a great one is available: "If a man who enjoys a lesser happiness beholds a greater one, let him leave aside the lesser to gain the greater."[25] If you will "vanquish the ego by yourself alone," then "[a]biding joy will be yours when all selfish desires end."[26]

Living well, then, is possible, but it requires using Zen training (or some similar meditation or body practice) to discipline the mind. How does this work?

5: Zen Training and Desire

Some outsiders have an appealing image of what Zen training is like. They think it must be quite peaceful and serene. They tend to imagine a cluster of robed adults sitting silently and harmoniously in some quiet rural setting until, one by one, somewhat like popping corn being heated, they individually burst awake. They imagine that attending a Zen retreat must be a wonderful escape from life.

Not!

Imagine, instead, that it's mid-afternoon on a hot summer's day. After sleeping less than four hours, you've already been awake for about twelve hours. You've eaten very little. You are sitting motionless on a cushion on a mat, but, even though you aren't moving, you can feel the sweat continuing to trickle down your face and legs. Even though you've had some breaks, after many hours of meditation the pain in your back and knees is becoming more and more relentless. You are able to hear noise from distant traffic, which you find quite distracting. If you are lucky, soon a monitor will come along to encourage you by striking you four times on your trapezius muscles with a stick. You know that you are supposed to be focusing on your practice, but your mind constantly drifts towards a shower followed by a massage, perhaps some good sex, and a long night's sleep. In other words, you'd rather be elsewhere.

The purpose of attending a retreat is to become more fully one with life.[27]

As one expert remarks, "Zen's reputation for being fierce, uncompromising, demanding, and painful at times is justly deserved."[28] It's not just humbling; it's humiliating.

We've seen that the purpose of Zen training is to teach us how to control our minds. It works because it provides **feedback** when we are misusing them. The difficulty comes from the fact that, in ordinary life, there seems to be no immediate penalty for indulging our proclivity for incessant conceptualizing. Permit me a concrete training example.

Zen training in Japan has traditionally occurred in temples that have a reputation for being dreadfully uncomfortable. Practitioners are given a bland diet mostly consisting of rice and vegetables. Temples are reported to be almost unbearably cold in winter and insufferably hot in summer. There are also stories like the one about a master who opened the screens while his students were seated in meditation so that they could become one with the mosquitoes.

Surely the Japanese have known for centuries how to build buildings that were warm in winter and cool in summer. I've visited Japan. Japanese chefs know how to cook delicious meals. The Japanese don't like being bitten by mosquitoes any more than we do. What's going on?

Consider this case: "A monk said to Tozan, 'Cold and heat descend upon us. How can we avoid them?' Tozan said, 'Why don't you go to where there is no cold or heat?' The monk said, 'Where is the place where there is no cold or heat?' Tozan said, 'When cold, let it be so cold that it kills you; when hot, let it be so hot that it kills you.'"[29]

Do you understand?

We all want to get to a place where there is no cold or heat. That's a place where, if cold, we can become warmer or, if hot, we can become cooler. In other words, it's a place where we have no desires. The master challenges us: why don't we go there?

Well, how do we get there?

We have to kill ourselves, in other words, we have to destroy our egos. We have to kill our egocentric likes and dislikes. Doing so leaves us with no desires.

As Jianzhi Sengcan (*d.* 606) says at the start of his great "Affirming Faith in Mind": "The Great Way is not difficult / for those who do not pick and choose. / When preferences are cast aside, / the Way stands clear and undisguised."[30]

Because they help us to let go of our egocentric preferences if we use them correctly, adverse conditions can actually help our training. Suppose, say, there's pain in my knees during a "round" of seated Zen training. What should I do? Until the round ends, I'm unable to get up and walk around to alleviate it. If I sit there and think about it, I'll become more miserable by becoming even more acutely aware of the pain. If, though, I simply accept it, if I give up thinking about it, I'll be able to focus more intensely on my practice, which, of course, is exactly what I should be doing. In this way, I would be practicing properly, strengthening my ability to focus attention to where I want it to be.

Let's connect this with the Buddha's innovative doctrine of <u>anatman,</u> no-self. In this case, my desire is to alleviate the pain in my knees.

Egoistic desires are either positive (attachments) or negative (aversions). There are all kinds of goods we typically desire, and there are all kinds of evils we typically try to avoid. This is **the way of the world**: ordinary life is a ceaseless quest to gain what we like and to avoid or lose what we don't like.

The Buddha says, "Don't follow the way of the world."[31] Instead of endlessly trying to possess what we like and to avoid what we don't like, we have seen how he thinks it much better to train our minds to let go of all egoistic desires.

Tozan understands that the monk's problem is not, for example, that he is too hot: it's that he desires not to be hot. He wants the world to be other than it is. The monk is carrying this burden. To free himself of it, Tozan recommends simply letting it go. The monk is actually making a problem where there isn't one. Without realizing it, he is preventing himself from living well.

Similarly, my problem isn't the pain in my knees. My problem is that I don't want the pain in my knees.

This brings us to a critical idea: according to the Buddha, we lack separate, independent selves. In fact, **nothing has a self**. "All states are without self; those who realize this are freed from suffering."[32] What does this mean?

It's impossible to desire something that one already has; it's only possible to desire what one lacks. Hunger, for example, is the desire for food. (Don't confuse the hunger with its object, namely, food. For example, while the consequences of actually ingesting food can be good, the only good with respect to the hunger itself is its annihilation.) When I'm hungry, I want to eat, I want to diminish the separation or gap between where I am and where I would like to be. I want the world to be different. It's the same with respect to the pain in my knees: I want it not to be as it is. When I have unsatisfied desires, I am dissatisfied. I am always finding myself dissatisfied about something; I am always lacking something. I want it to be cooler or to feel less pain or to eat.

Yes, that's the appearance, but it's not—according to the Buddha—the reality. I lack nothing. It's a delusion that I lack anything. There really is no genuine separation between me and everything else. There's never any need to be dissatisfied. (Don't confuse dissatisfaction or suffering with feeling pain. It's probably impossible to live without feeling pain; pain is a condition of being alive. Rather, the Buddha (Gotama) teaches how to reduce and eliminate cure dissatisfaction, how to end suffering.) **No separation, no dissatisfaction.**

The purpose of Zen training is to realize this. In other words, it's to free oneself from dissatisfaction or suffering. We are unintentionally causing ourselves to suffer—incessantly.

The only good desire is a non-egocentric desire, and the only non-egocentric desire is the desire to get rid of egoistic desires, in other words, the desire to awaken and become enlightened.

So how does successful Zen training kill egocentric desires like hunger or lust? How could it possibly end suffering? How could anything end dissatisfaction?

6: How Zen Training Works

There are many kinds of Buddhist meditation techniques. The three classic ones in Zen training are [i] counting inhalations and exhalations, [ii] counting exhalations, and [iii] following the breath. The first two are most useful for beginners. Following the breath is the one that the Buddha himself used to free himself from conditioning. Unfortunately, it's as difficult as it is simple.

Perhaps for that reason, for about the last 1500 years another technique has been developed that has proven quite effective, namely, koan training.

As an introduction, consider this Japanese story retold by Stephen Mitchell:

"A hundred and fifty years ago there lived a woman named Sono, whose devotion and purity of heart were respected far and wide. One day a fellow Buddhist, having made a long trip to see her, asked, 'What can I do to put my heart at rest?' She said, 'Every morning and every evening, and whenever anything happens to you, keep on saying, "Thanks for everything. I have no complaint whatsoever."' The man did as he was instructed, for a whole year, but his heart was still not at peace. He returned to Sono, crestfallen. 'I've said your prayer over and over, and yet nothing in my life has changed; I'm still the same selfish person as before. What should I do now?' Sono immediately said, 'Thanks for everything. I have no complaint whatsoever.' On hearing these words, the man was able to open his spiritual eye, and returned home with great joy."

In Chinese, 'kung-an' means 'public cases.' Koans are enigmatic, seemingly absurd utterances and gestures understood to be expressions of enlightened minds that are used as training tools designed to provoke awakening. They are often considered the most distinctive characteristic of Zen training and thought. Instead of discussing them abstractly, permit me simply to provide a concrete example (as well as to recommend some readings in case you have further interest[33]).

Here's the most popular koan given to Zen students who are ripe to go past a counting practice: "A monk in all seriousness asked Zhaozhou [Josho (778-897)], 'Does a dog have Buddha nature or not?' Zhaozhou retorted, 'Mu.'" That's all there is to the famous koan Mu.

According to Buddhist teaching ("the Dharma"), it seems both wrong to claim that a dog has Buddha nature and wrong to say that a dog fails to have Buddha nature. Zhaozhou's response points beyond both possible conceptual answers. "Mu" is a signpost to the Unconditioned [see the next section]. In other words, Zhaozhou is inviting the monk to let go of conceptualizing, to stop thinking about how to conceptualize other sentient animals correctly.

So? How does Mu help a contemporary practitioner?

What a student who is assigned Mu does is to work on it simply by focusing on the word 'Mu' itself. Instead of trying to think of a rational solution, the challenge for the student is to let go of thinking about Mu (in other words, making judgments related to Mu) and simply remain noticing 'Mu.' Let's analyze this.

Let's break down the usual idea of a human life as one that lasts for some decades. Let's agree that a whole life is composed of thousands of "mini-lives", namely, breaths. Each breath begins in silence and ends in silence; the inhalation comes from silence and the exhalation returns to silence. For a Zen student working on Mu, a perfect mini-life would be one focused on <u>Mu</u> continuously for the duration of that single breath. Similarly, working on <u>Mu</u> perfectly for half an hour would be focusing on <u>Mu</u> continuously for thirty minutes without interruption.

For how long does a Zen student need to work on <u>Mu</u>? For however long it takes—a week, a few decades, whatever. Trying to break past it previously doesn't count at all; only breaking past it counts. In Yasutani-Roshi's commentary on <u>Mu</u>, he says, "You must not practice fitfully... You must carry on steadfastly for one, two, three, or even five years without remission, constantly vigilant."[34]

He's talking about working on <u>Mu</u> during all one's waking moments.

The idea is to use the focus of practicing to replace the constant conceptualizing or mental chatter that is otherwise always the background noise of life. Instead of letting the running commentary or story continue endlessly, the task is to let it vanish simply by noticing <u>Mu</u> continuously.

The fewer distractions one has, the easier it is not to be separated from <u>Mu</u>. Since sitting perfectly still generates fewer distractions than walking, being motionless is preferable to moving in terms of working on <u>Mu</u>. Moving by walking clockwise at a slow, uniform speed over a familiar course with eyes lowered is preferable to moving in any other fashion. Nothing is as distracting as talking with, or listening to, others—though, eventually, even that can be done. (Master meditators are always meditating.) So another reason to go on Zen training retreats (<u>sesshin</u>) is to work harder on one's practice by deliberately reducing distractions.

To work on a koan is simply to pay attention to it, to notice it continuously throughout each breath. One drops one's practice whenever one gets distracted and begins again to make judgments. "Thought trains," judgments that follow related judgments, always lead away from one's practice. In effect, then, the task is to become a <u>Mu</u> simpleton.

This task is difficult for everyone. It's especially difficult for intellectuals. For example, a professor who makes a living learning, talking about, evaluating, writing about, and revising judgments typically has a more difficult time awakening than, say, someone who is illiterate and not obsessed with trafficking in ideas. On the other hand, when intellectuals do awaken, they often awaken more completely.[35] Therefore, there need be no rush to awaken. **When the mind is completely empty of judgments, awakening will occur.** In fact, a thorough, delayed awakening is preferable to a shallow, quick one.

As usual in the context of mastery[36], techniques are overrated. All that matters is noticing <u>Mu</u> during both the inhalation and the exhalation. It doesn't even matter if different sensory modalities are used. For example, visualizing the word '<u>Mu</u>' during inhalation and imagining hearing the sound of saying '<u>Mu</u>' during exhalation are perfectly acceptable together. As often as possible, it's best to keep <u>Mu</u> in the "forefront" of consciousness, but, when necessary outside formal sitting, it's acceptable simply to keep it in the "back" of the mind as long as one keeps it there continuously.

There are many traps in spiritual training. Here are three. One is the all-or-nothing trap: it's thinking that either I am awakened or my practice is useless. The problem with that trap is that it involves judging (thinking, conceptualizing). Accept that, if you are working on your practice, your practice is working on you, and just keep working. Another is the trap of thinking that, since I've not broken through yet, my technique must be wrong. Again, the problem with this trap is that it involves judging. If you are refusing to become separated from <u>Mu</u> during both the inhalation and the exhalation, your technique is fine. A third is the trap of thinking that you are doing worse or better than some other student. Again, the problem with that trap is that comparisons involve judging. As always, as soon as you notice that you are again judging, drop the judging and return to practicing.

Traps may be understood as efforts by the ego/I to prevent its own annihilation. The same may be true for much of the pain one experiences when practicing formally.

These difficulties are important reasons why even Thich Nhat Hanh, who some Zen masters have actually called a "liar" because he makes living well seem so easy, writes that "Practicing meditation . . . is very difficult."[37] **Zen training is simple and very difficult.** It's theoretically possible for all of us to awaken, but there is no guarantee that any particular individual can ever do it. The most important qualities to achieving the primary benefits seem to be intensity and perseverance. As Roshi Kapleau points out, mastering Zen training "is like learning anything valuable. It calls for perserverance."[38]

It's critical that working on <u>Mu</u> is merely noticing <u>Mu</u>. It is not thinking about <u>Mu</u> or anything else. There has to be a complete absence of conceptualizing, of judgment mongering, for awakening to occur. It's like noticing the corner of the table (from a previous example) continuously. Doing this fosters the precondition of awakening, which is a "clean slate" mind, in other words, one completely empty of judgments.[39]

The more attention we expend on something, the more important it becomes.

So, the more attention a Zen student expends on noticing <u>Mu</u>, the more important it becomes. If one concentrates on <u>Mu</u> intensely enough long enough, according to Master Mumon, "It will be just as if you swallow a red-hot iron ball, which you cannot spit out even if you try."[40] You'll be stuck. You won't be able to vomit the ball out or let it stay where it is. Mumon says, "Employ every ounce of your energy to work on this 'Mu'."

Why? It's because the more you work on **Mu**, the more it will expand in importance. If you keep working on it, eventually it **will crowd out all judgments from the mind**. When your mind becomes empty of all judgments for a single moment, you'll realize your true nature. You'll achieve a spiritual breakthrough. You'll awaken. Instead of trying to live well, from then on your only task will be continuing to live better and better (by, in koan training, continuing to work on additional koans and letting the resulting insight permeate your life).

This explanation has the virtue of not only explaining koan training, but also of being easily extended to explain other kinds of spiritual trainings or body practices. It is not, for example, necessary to use koan training to achieve a breakthrough; other kinds of mantras in addition to koans can work. Getting attached to any view (for example, that my practice is the best kind of practice for everyone) is the greatest spiritual trap of all.

This explanation also shows how koan training works. Specifically, it is <u>not</u> a matter of trying to expel all judgments. It's a matter of focusing solely on the koan and allowing it to work its magic.

It also explains why, especially at the beginning, working on a koan is so difficult. It's not merely that it requires intense, persistent practice. It's that it requires an obsessiveness that is initially very difficult to muster.

Consider an analogy. Imagine (or, in cases like mine, remember) a teenage boy in an identity crisis initially confronting the important existential questions. He asks: Who am I? What am I doing here? How did I get here? What should I be doing? What will happen to me? Our boy falls head over heels in love with a girl. When he isn't with her, he thinks about her constantly. He wakes up in the morning with her on his mind and she's the object of his last thoughts at night. He lives for those precious moments when they are together. He fears that rejection by her would kill him. He becomes quite mad. In short, he is obsessed.

Especially if the girl is beautiful and sexually desirable, such an obsession is easily imaginable. It's certainly more positively intense than confronting the existential questions in solitude. Notice, too, that he doesn't have to be taught the correct technique for being obsessive.

By way of contrast, imagine becoming obsessed by Mu. It is a gateway to the Unconditioned, but the Zen student initially only thinks that instead of having directly experienced it. It seems to be nothing but an arbitrary, meaningless, foreign word. There's nothing beautiful or sexy about it! It cannot kiss or hug or love you back. The truth is that one may have to force oneself into becoming obsessed with it.

According to Roshi Kapleau, few people are sufficiently obsessed. Only a handful of people are really driven. To make this point, he more than once in his books repeats this concrete life-or-death analogy: "'To come to full awakening,' as one Zen master put it, 'you must act like a man who has fallen into a hundred-foot-deep pit. His thousand, his ten thousand thoughts are reduced to the single thought: "How can I get out of this pit?" He keeps it up from morning to night and from night to the following morning with no other thought.'"[41] In traditional terms, one-pointedness is required for awakening.

This is why, if your goal is to enjoy the primary benefits, it's important to have sufficiently strong motivation when beginning Zen training. If you don't really fear death or really want to understand your true nature or really want to help others, you'll have insufficient motivation to awaken. When it becomes difficult to be obsessed by a koan, you won't become obsessed by it. Instead of noticing it for the whole of each breath, you'll revert to judging, which prevents awakening. One's attitude should be like the Buddha's: either awakening or death.

7: Conditioned / Unconditioned

The teachings of various Zen masters are often systematically misleading in an instructive way. It's helpful to understand this. To do that, let's roughly distinguish two ways of looking at what-is. Let's call one 'conditioned' and the other 'unconditioned.'

The Conditioned / The Unconditioned

multiplicity /   unity
temporality / eternity
motion / rest
dynamic / static
noise / silence
becoming / being
form (body) / emptiness
limited / limitless
perception / conception
desire / fulfillment
war / peace
egocentric / egoless
incomplete / complete
causality / no causality
relative / absolute
appearance / reality

Philosophers (people who seriously seek to live well, fundamental thinkers [see my The Meditative Approach to Philosophy or Mastery in 7 Steps]) from both the western and eastern traditions are familiar with this basic distinction. Western thinkers who have discussed it include Parmenides, Plato, Plotinus, Eckhart, Spinoza, and Bradley.

Once this distinction is articulated even roughly, the question that may be asked is: "Is Zen training based on the Unconditioned?" Judging from emphasis of many Zen teachers, the answer would naturally seem to be, "Yes."

It is this answer, though, that is misleading. It's instructive to understand why it's misleading. Why do many Zen teachers emphasize the Unconditioned? It's not because they are attached to the Unconditioned as opposed to the Conditioned. It's because most Zen students are attached to the Conditioned, and, so, to rectify the imbalance, Zen teachers often emphasize the Unconditioned rather than the Conditioned. Since students are typically already attached to it, the Conditioned doesn't need additional emphasis.

Here's the chief point: what-is is both the Conditioned and the Unconditioned. When Jianzhi Sengcan talks in "Affirming Faith in Mind" about apprehending everything with "equal mind," he's referring to the harmony of the Conditioned and the Unconditioned. **Without gratuitous evaluations, the mind is centered and perfectly balanced.**

Using traditional terminology, samsara is the conditioned domain and nirvana is the unconditioned domain. The truth, which can shock, is that **samsara is nirvana.**

There is one reality, but there are two ways of apprehending it, namely, from the Conditioned and from the Unconditioned. It's a bit like having one coin that can be seen from either the heads side or the tails side. Yes, there's only one heads side, and, yes, there's only one tails side; however, though there are two sides, there's still only one coin.

This is a point that philosophers who are mystics or monists have repeatedly made. It is why conceptualization is, ultimately, misleading.

Answer quickly: is the world red or not? Quick!

Since many real objects are not red, don't answer that the world is red. Since many real objects are red, don't answer that it's false that the world is red. It would also be misleading to answer that the world is neither red nor not red or to answer that the world is both red and not red.

The problem comes because one is mixing the level of the whole with the level of the parts in one judgment. As a whole, the world is beyond red and not red; however, some parts of the world are red and it's false that other parts of the world are red.

Is a whole its parts? Well, yes and no. This is the glory and misery of conceptualization.[42]

The shift in perspective removes the problem. There's no problem on the whole level or on the parts level; there's only a problem when the two levels are mixed.

When noticing a koan sufficiently results in a radical shift in mind-set, there's no problem. The elusive becomes obvious. The appearance of incoherence or absurdity with respect to the koan instantly vanishes. There never was a real problem; instead, there was a conceptual problem. It's like a gestalt drawing of a duck/rabbit or an old woman/young woman. What is the subject of the drawing? There's one answer when looked at one way, another answer when looked at in another way. There's no real problem as long as the two perspectives (levels, interpretations) are not confused.

This is why Daido Roshi rejects the common view of koans as paradoxes: "Paradox exists only in language, in the words and ideas that describe reality. In reality itself there are no paradoxes."[43] The answer to a koan is never a single judgment but a state of mind. To solve one's first koan is to awaken.

A student working on Mu keeps wondering, "What is Mu?" The student assumes that he is a subject wondering about something else, a different object. Well, yes, that is one perspective. On the other hand, the only gap is in the student's apprehension, in other words, the student is Mu! Focusing on Mu is focusing on your own name. You already are what you are trying to understand. The putative gap is a delusion due to a certain deluded state of mind caused by attachment to the ego/I. It's a matter of difference-in-identity.[44] As long as one stays stuck conceptualizing Mu, there's a problem. Once one lets go of conceptualizing it, there's no problem.

One master puts it this way: "While we are fully aware of and observing deeply an object, the boundary between the subject who observes and the object being observed gradually dissolves, and the subject and object become one. This is the essence of meditation."[45]

The importance of directly experiencing this (as opposed merely to thinking about it) cannot be overemphasized. Let's relate this first to the self and then to desiring.

First, the separate self disappears. I am not only impermanent but also empty! This is no mere thought: it's the way it is. There is no longer any gap between me and everything else. I am everything else; there's no separation. I am intimately connected to everything else. Similarly, nothing else has a separate self either. Every other individual is also empty of a separate self and devoid of permanence.

Second, realizing (not merely thinking!) the truth of this perspective immediately undermines all desires. If I am impermanent and empty, how could I grasp anything else? If everything else is also impermanent and empty, how could anything else be grasped? Right here, right now, there is everything necessary.

This explains why Nhich Nhat Hanh wrote: "If you are not satisfied with what is available in the present moment, you will never be satisfied by attaining what you think will bring you happiness in the future."[46]

Since suffering or dissatisfaction depends upon a separation between where I am and where I want to be, if I am already everything, I cannot really suffer. Of course, it's possible to think that I am suffering, but that's just as false as thinking that I am a separate self. The Buddha's original doctrine of anatman, then, is the critical element in understanding how Zen training can dissolve all suffering. **Emptiness permits fullness.**

8: Is Zen Training For You?

If you are sufficiently interested in one or more of the secondary benefits and willing to train daily for half an hour (and an hour would be much, much better), then the answer is an unqualified "Yes." It's definitely a life-enhancing skill that can be quickly learned.

In my personal experience as well as according to the testimony of some others, it typically seems to require about 45 minutes or so for judgments to begin to settle noticeably. Therefore, I suggest aiming for two consecutive rounds of twenty-five (or thirty) minutes of formal seated training daily.

This, though, is far too much for a beginner. Just begin slowly, and naturally and gradually extend the duration of your sitting daily over some months until you reach at least this suggested duration. Keep your intensity of focus as high as possible for whatever duration you select. You may have a brief walking meditation between rounds—and keep practicing during the walking. Once you are doing that daily, I predict that you'll notice subtle but significant improvements in, for example, how calm you generally feel. In other words, you'll soon begin to experience and appreciate the secondary benefits.

Here's how to get started. If you happen to have Zen training center near you, contact them to see if an introductory workshop is offered.[47] Alternatively (or in addition), there are excellent books available that will enable you to get started on your own. The best is Philip Kapleau's The Three Pillars of Zen (2nd ed.). [I provide clear, step-by-step instructions in my much shorter The Meditative Approach to Philosophy and other books.]

There's no reason why anyone interested in any of the secondary benefits should not learn how to meditate. The benefits enormously exceed the costs.

Yes, it does have costs. Time spent in formal Zen training is time that cannot be spent doing anything else. Furthermore, if you don't join a training center, which will have yearly dues, you'll need to purchase some equipment for training at home. At a minimum, you'll need a cushion or a bench and a timer. It would also be best to have a mat and a robe. You may also want a bell or incense or some other implements that may enhance practicing.

If you are interested in the primary benefits, you may begin in any of the ways just described, but you'll need to find a suitable teacher sooner rather than later. Unless you are a spiritual genius like the Buddha and willing to let everything else in life go to achieve a breakthrough, you should no more expect to teach yourself how to awaken spiritually than you should expect to teach yourself how to become a world class figure skater or golfer.[48]

The spiritual journey is not to be undertaken lightly. Why? It's a journey that will last the rest of your life. No matter how well you practice, the rest of your days may be too few for awakening. Even if you awaken, you will need all your remaining days to work on becoming more enlightened. My suggestion, again, is not to begin until you are really ready, fully ripe. When you become sufficiently tired of so much dissatisfaction that you realize that you need a significant change, seize that moment to begin.

If you are not particularly interested in the primary benefits but are seriously interested in living the most ethical life possible, it's important not to delay the start of the journey too long. As the Buddha claimed and for reasons that I have given elsewhere[49], it's not just that living well is impossible without enlightenment, it's that living well includes living ethically. In other words, it is not possible to live ethically without enlightenment.[50]

So it's important to <u>determine in advance what you are trying to do.</u> Initially, as Roshi Kapleau points out, "you must decide what it is you want and what you are prepared to work hard for. Ask yourself . . . 'Do I really yearn to know who I am, why I was born, why I must die, what the meaning of my life is? Or is my aim simply to tone up my body, improve my concentration, or learn to relax?'"[51] Your goal will determine how you should proceed.

Most koan training is informal rather than formal. A practitioner may train formally for only an hour or so daily, but, ideally, informal koan training should continue through all one's waking hours. Informal koan training is compatible with our usual tasks such as working, exercising, washing, and relaxing. In fact, by reducing the role of the ego/I, it makes them all more satisfying. This is what it means to claim that Zen training is a way of life.

9: Mistakes that Zen Trainers Make

The work of a Zen trainer is to encourage as many students as possible to awaken and to increase the depths of their [the students'] enlightenment.

Teaching what cannot be conceptualized is extremely odd work![52] Your Zen teacher cannot teach you, say, the meaning of <u>Mu</u> because, it, "like every Zen koan, is thrusting truth at you, truth that cannot be taught but must be caught."[53] It cannot be taught, because, since conceptual understanding works dualistically by dividing, **unity cannot be understood conceptually**. It's impossible to divide unity. It can, however, be caught in the sense that unity can be experienced directly.

In addition to showing students how to live, in other words, in addition to teaching by example, Zen teachers may be unable to talk intelligibly about the primary benefits of Zen training (because of the impossibility of conceptualizing unity) but they are able to talk about how to practice well.

Unfortunately, in their zeal to communicate how important those primary benefits are, they often put the emphasis of their remarks in the wrong place. If your teacher happens to be one who makes this error, please don't let it undermine your confidence.

In talking to students who are already practicing, Zen trainers can either (A) emphasize the importance of continuing to work towards awakening, which is what they tend to do, or they can (B) talk about how far the students have already progressed, which is what they don't tend to do.

Of course it's important to try to talk about the primary benefits of Zen training, but they should talk much more frequently than they actually do about the secondary benefits. If so, alternative B is preferable to A. The reason for this is psychological.

Consider an analogy. Imagine yourself coaching a losing high school football team. Would the members of your team practice more intensely (and, so, be more likely to begin winning) if you (A) kept emphasizing how far they were from playing well or if you (B) kept reminding them about how much progress they had already made (even though they haven't yet begun to win many or even any games)? B is the correct answer. Why?

To use alternative A would be to emphasize the gap between where they are now and where they have to go. The more the players think about the gap, the more important it becomes. The more they think about it, the more likely they are to think of themselves as failures, as unable ever to cross that imposing divide. Soon, playing football well may seem as unattainable as running fast enough to reach the horizon.

To use alternative B would be to emphasize what they are already doing well. Suppose, for example, that an excellent running back has to master five specific skills and that you are coaching a running back who has mastered only one of the five. By emphasizing that he has already mastered one, you offer genuine hope that he can master another—and perhaps even another after that. After all, if he mastered one task, why couldn't he master another? If, on the other hand, you constantly tell him what he already knows, namely, that he has not yet mastered four of the five skills required, he'll eventually begin to wonder if he has already reached his limit. So, emphasize what he is already doing correctly—and keep being positive rather than negative.

Now imagine yourself a Zen teacher at a retreat. Should you constantly be telling your students that they are not working hard enough, that the distance between where they are and awakening is still enormous? Alternatively, should you constantly be telling your students that they are already doing a lot right, that they are already on the right path?

Well, if they are already on retreat, already sitting formally for ten hours daily, already observing silence between themselves, already doing with less sleep than normal, already separated from their friends and family, and so on, they are already, in fact, doing a lot right. If so, emphasize that. Keep being positive.

Instead of talking about the glorious life without dissatisfaction that awaits them after awakening, emphasize how they already are enjoying some of the secondary benefits of their practice. This approach will help them feel as if they are already making progress and, so, surely, they'll be able to make more.

In other words, it alleviates the problem of measuring progress. It's always easier to improve what can be measured than to improve what cannot be measured. A very serious problem with traditional Zen training is that there seems to be no way to measure any progress once a student begins until awakening. In other words, it's too all or nothing.

I'm not denying the reality! I'm claiming that Zen teachers needlessly overstate it. More than once I've read of a teacher who tells Zen students that "real" Zen training doesn't even begin until awakening.[54] Imagine that you have been a serious Zen student for ten years working on your practice as well as you seem able to work and then your teacher tells you that you haven't yet begun to practice seriously. Most students would be so discouraged that they'd be tempted to quit.

The alternative is to use, however imperfectly, the secondary benefits as measuring devices. Have students focus on, for example, how much calmer they already feel after having practiced for just a few months. Have them notice how much more quickly they fall asleep at night. Have them notice how much more deeply they sleep and, perhaps, how much less time they have to spend sleeping. Have them notice how much easier it is for them to say "no" to desserts. Have them notice how much more quickly the rounds of sitting seem to go during a retreat. Have them notice that there are more "spaces" between thoughts. And so on. Most students would be so encouraged by realizing the progress they'd already made that they'd become more confident and even eager to find ways to practice more effectively.

Like the rest of us, Zen teachers can get attached to familiar procedures. The best Zen teachers are open to new techniques. For example, it will soon be possible, if it isn't already, to use EEG machines to provide more precise feedback. It's easy to imagine a machine that records a practitioner's brain waves as that practitioner focuses on, say, <u>Mu</u>. Have the machine "remember" the relevant pattern, and use the machine while seated in formal Zen training to detect significant deviations that would occur in the brain's electrical field when the practitioner reverts to making judgments. As soon as the practitioner loses focus, a mild electrical shock could follow. That more precise feedback mechanism might well shorten the training time required for awakening.

What about objections to serious Zen training, in other words, training aimed at the primary benefits? Objections from the ignorant and the lazy should simply be ignored. Even objections concerning awakening are not troublesome. As previously noted, unless they are expanded by continued training, awakenings are nothing but interesting experiences. The only objection that would be troublesome would be one from someone who might be called a deeply realized person, in other words, someone who had not only awakened but significantly expanded awakening by further training. Though there could be such an objection, I have never come across one—and I've done a lot of looking. Please correct me if you discover that I'm wrong, but there appears to be no such thing as a deeply realized person who recommends against Zen training.[55]

There's a difference between a good life and a great one. Good is the enemy of great. None of us has to settle for a good life. We all have the opportunity for a great life. Why not go for it? If you do, I wish you well.

Notes

1. Sigmund Freud, Civilization and Its Discontents (N.Y.: Norton, 1961; James Strachey, tr.), p. 22.

2. Civilization and Its Discontents, p. 22.

3. For a short survey of theories of human nature, see Leslie Stevenson and David L. Haberman's Ten Theories of Human Nature. Many philosophers have noted the connection between axiological theories and theories of human nature. For example, "Many of the really difficult questions at the roots of economic disputes concern differing conceptions of human needs" C. Dyke, Philosophy of Economics (Englewood Cliffs, N.J.: Prentice-Hall, 1981), p. 19. Conceptions of human needs depend, of course, upon conceptions of human nature.

4. Much of my understanding of Zen training, such as this recipe, is due to my association with The Venerable Bodhin Kjolhede, Roshi, over the last 20+ years. Frankly, I cannot often remember whether I first understood something from listening to or observing Roshi, experiencing it myself, or absorbing it from another master's writings. Suffice it to say that, without his guidance, my understanding, which is still weak, would be even weaker.

5. Thich Nhat Hanh: "Practicing Buddhism is a clever way to enjoy life."

6. Some may object that this violates Brentano's thesis of the intentionality of consciousness, which is that every episode of consciousness has some object or other: "Every mental phenomenon is characterized by what the Scholastics . . . called the intentional (or mental) inexistence of an object . . . Every mental phenomenon includes something as object within itself" [Franz Brentano, Psychology from an Empirical Standpoint

[N.Y.: Humanities, 1973] p. 88.). The answer to the objection is that not all objects are judgments. In other words, it's possible to empty the mind of all judgments without emptying it of all objects.

7. He seems to have spoken Magadhan, which is close to Pali, a north Indian dialect.

8. A popular recent biography by an outsider is Karen Armstrong's Buddha (N.Y.: Penguin, 2001). A fine biography by an insider is Thich Nhat Hanh's Old Path White Clouds: Walking in the Footsteps of the Buddha (Berkeley, California: Parallax, 1991).

9. Cf. Huston Smith's The World's Religions (N.Y.: Harper Collins, 1958 & 1991), Chapter III.

10. The Buddha, The Dhammapada (Tomales, California: Nilgiri, 1985; Eknath Easwaran, tr.), p. 87. 'Dhammapada' means 'the path of the dharma' or teaching. It's a collection of the Buddha's sayings. I also recommend Early Buddhist Discourses (Indianapolis: Hackett, 2006), edited and translated by John J. Holder. It's more systematic than The Dhammapada. I highly recommend two other recent anthologies: Bhikkhu Bodhi, ed., In the Buddha's Words and Glenn Wallis, ed., Basic Teachings of the Buddha.

11. The Dhammapada, pp. 88 & 125.

12. The Dhammapada, p. 132. Cf. the section that follows below on The Conditioned and the Unconditioned.

13. The Dhammapada, pp. 143 & 148.

14. The Dhammapada, p. 149.

15. The Dhammapada, pp. 163 & 193. My emphasis.

16. The Dhammapada, p. 167.

17. The Dhammapada, pp. 176-7.

18. The Dhammapada, p. 185.

19. The Dhammapada, p. 186.

20. The Dhammapada, pp.192 & 193.

21. The Dhammapada, p. 194.

22. The Dhammapada, p. 195.

23. The Dhammapada, p. 96.

24. The Dhammapada, p. 78.

25. The Dhammapada, p. 167.

26. The Dhammapada, p. 169. Notice "abiding": this is not the joy that alternates with sorrow. It is unending bliss, nirvana.

27. ZEN Merging of East and West (N.Y.: Doubleday, 1979), p. 221.

28. Tensho David Schneider in Kazuaki Tanahashi and Tensho David Schneider, Essential Zen (Edison, New Jersey: Castle, 1994), p. XIII.

29. This is case 43 from Hekiganroku. Katsuki Sekida, Two Zen Classics (N.Y.: Weatherhill, 1977), p. 267.

30. Chants & Recitations (Rochester, New York: Rochester Zen Center, 2005), p. 25. Two outstanding sources of information on the ancient Chinese patriarchs are John C. H. Wu's The Golden Age of Zen (N.Y.: Doubleday, 1996) and Andy Ferguson's Zen's Chinese Heritage (Boston: Wisdom, 2000). There have been many great Buddhist thinkers such as Nagarjuna, Shantideva, and Dogen who have given us inspiring works. Even today there are contemporary authors who provide continuing inspiration (such as, just to mention a specific example of one I read recently, Ajahn Sumedho's The Way It Is).

31. The Dhammapada, p. 125.

32. The Dhammapada, p. 163.

33. Steven Heine's Opening A Mountain (N.Y.: Oxford University Press, 2002), Philip Kapleau's Straight to the Heart of Zen (Boston: Shambhala, 2001), John Daido Loori, ed., Sitting With Koans (Boston: Wisdom, 2006), and Steven Heine and Dale S. Wright, eds., The Koan (New York: Oxford University Press, 2000). It's fine to read about koans on your own, but please do not assign one to yourself.

34. Roshi Philip Kapleau, The Three Pillars of Zen (N.Y.: Doubleday, 1965), p. 84.

35. For more on this topic, see ZEN Merging of East and West, p. 120.

36. See my Mastery in 7 Steps, Chapter 10.

37. Thich Nhat Hanh, Being Peace (Berkeley, California: Parallax, 1987), p. 8.

38. ZEN Merging of East and West, p. 59.

39. ZEN Merging of East and West, p. 137.

40. Two Zen Classics, p. 28.

41. ZEN Merging of East and West, p. 50.

42. For an excellent discussion of the part/whole analogy, see Panayot Butchvarov, "The Limits of Ontological Analysis," in M. S. Gram and E. D. Klemke, eds., The Ontological Turn (Iowa City: University of Iowa Press, 1974).

43. John Daido Loori, ed., Sitting with Koans (Boston: Wisdom, 2006), p. 1.

44. The best recent work on the concept of identity has been done by Panayot Butchvarov. In particular, see Being Qua Being: A Theory of Identity, Existence, and Predication (Bloomington: Indiana University Press, 1979) (especially the first three chapters) and Skepticism about the External World (N.Y.: Oxford University Press, 1998) (especially Chapter 6).

45. Thich Nhat Hanh, Transformation & Healing (Berkeley, California: Parallax, 1990), p. 38. Notice that he does not state that while meditating we are judging or thinking about the object.

46. Thich Naht Hanh, Breathe! You Are Alive (Berkeley, California: Paralax, 1996), p. 82. Years ago when I first read it, this sentence really helped open my understanding. Compare: "Emptiness is a way of expressing that all species exist in connection with and in

dependence upon each other" [Thich Nhat Hanh, The Blooming of a Lotus (Boston: Beacon, 1993), p. 122.

47. The Rochester Zen Center offers an excellent one; it's always given on a Saturday about once every two months.

48. Finding a suitable teacher is no easy task, and it's beyond the scope of this essay to consider it.

49. "Beyond Skepticism in Ethics" in Larry Lee Blackman, ed., The Philosophy of Panayot Butchvarov (Lewiston, N.Y.: Edwin Mellen, 2005).

50. Cf. John Daido Loori, Invoking Reality (Mt. Tremper, N.Y.: Dharma Communications, 1998.). Also see my Love and Respect.

51. ZEN Merging of East and West, p. 15.

52. Cf. Bonnie Myotai Treace's remark that "Zen teachers . . . have. . .the oddest job around: teach what cannot be taught" from John Daido Loori's The Eight Gates of Zen (Mt. Tremper, N.Y.: Dharma Communications, 1992), p. XI.

53. ZEN Merging of East and West, p. 81.

54. ZEN Merging of East and West, p. 30.

55. I thank Panayot Butchvarov, Dave Pascale, Art Spring, and Anna Wright for their comments on an earlier draft this work.

Appendix

Here are answers to some important questions that you may have. [They have been added for the second edition.]

Question: I've tried various meditation techniques before without success. Why haven't they worked?

An obvious explanation is that you didn't execute them properly. However, before you blame yourself, let me emphasize that there may have been nothing wrong at all with what you did. Why?

Usually, meditation techniques fail. It's instructive to understand why.

Spiritual or meditation techniques are designed to free the practitioner from excessive thinking. Following Roshi Kapleau let's call all thinking that involves nothing but repetitive useless thoughts "thoughting." There's nothing at all wrong with thinking, but thoughting, attachment to thinking, obstructs living well.

Therefore, the elimination of thoughting is required for living well. It's the primary aim of all spiritual or meditation techniques, all body practices, including zazen meditation.

Of course meditation techniques do not always fail. For some practitioners, occasionally, they work. There are no reliable statistics.

My guess? If 250 people practiced some standard meditative technique properly every day for one year, perhaps 1 or 2 would breakthrough and directly experience "no-thought," which is the elimination of thoughting. (This does not mean, however, that many more people wouldn't succeed with respect to the secondary goals. Perhaps nearly all would succeed in that sense. Meditation techniques almost always work to achieve their secondary purposes.) The focus here is only on their primary raison d'etre.

Why do meditation techniques usually fail with respect to their primary purposes?

It's ultimately because we are stuck identifying with our egos (self-concepts, ego-I's). We are, in other words, attached to thinking.

The ego thinks in terms of gains and losses. When meditation techniques are used for secondary purposes, for common mastery, the ego accepts them. Why? Becoming a master meditator takes years and years. Success is taken to be a future event, a special state of mind that may or may not occur at some later time.

If achieving this special state of mind called "awakening" is your aim, you'll never awaken. You may enjoy many of the secondary benefits of practicing meditation, but you won't wake up spiritually, you won't eliminate thoughting.

This is because it's impossible to think your way out of thoughting. If you think of awakening as a future goal to be achieved by mastering a meditation technique, it will always remain a goal to be achieved in the future, which means you'll never awaken because the future is never present.

As Helen Schucman's A Course in Miracles puts it: "[A] lifetime of contemplation and long periods of meditation . . .look to the future for release from a state of present unworthiness and inadequacy." Doing that is senseless, which explains why meditation techniques normally fail.

Again according to <u>A Course in Miracles</u>, the solution is simple: "Do not be concerned with time." With respect to the past, that's easy in theory because "The past is nothing . . . for the past is gone." With respect to the future, that, too, is easy in theory because the future is always future. It never arrives. It is never experienced. It's a set of thoughts. Obviously, it's impossible therefore to experience release from dissatisfaction in the future. Attempting to do it is senseless, which is why meditation techniques normally fail.

As Eckhart Tolle helpfully emphasizes, this passage from <u>A Course in Miracles</u> is the key: "it takes no time at all to be what you are."

As long as you remain attached to the thought that you are a temporal entity, that attachment will obstruct awakening. Any meditation technique you use will likely fail.

"Time is a belief of the ego." As long as you are attached to the thought that you are the ego, that attachment will obstruct awakening.

So the task is to drop identification with the ego.

Notice that the ego lives in the past or in the future; the present moment has no reality for the ego. The mind is always at a loss in the present moment; it is restless, bored, and eager to escape elsewhere.

"[T]he ego regards the present only as a brief transition to the future, in which it brings the past to the future by interpreting the present in past terms." Because it interprets the present moment in past terms, it keeps you bound, stuck, imprisoned. "'Now' has no meaning to the ego . . .Unless you learn that past is an illusion, you are choosing a future of illusions . . ."

The only time we have to live is the present moment, which the ego can't handle. What does this tell you about the ego? It's simple: "the ego is not sane."

If you are normal, your whole life is centered around the ego: all your beliefs, habits, and relationships. This explains why dissatisfaction is normal. "[E]veryone identifies himself with his thought system, and every thought system conters on what you believe you are . . . But if a lie is at its center, only deception proceeds from it." This is why your life has been so chaotic, insane, and dysfunctional. Until you awaken, your life is centered around a lie.

What has resulted from this? Delusive living. "It has taken time to misguide you so completely . . ." You have not only taken years to construct a thought system that seems to work for you, but you have also used it as the foundation for continuing to make decisions to construct your life.

"[N]ow is the release from time."

What can you do to make that release? Well, in a sense there's nothing that can be done. Trying to do something would just be setting up another goal to be realized in the future. This is why Sengcan, the third Zen ancestor, says in *Affirming Faith in Mind*: "The wise do not strive after goals; / the foolish put themselves in bonds." [Rochester Zen Center translation.]

There's nothing to do. There's nothing to seek. There's nowhere to look. Why?

You already are everything you need to be.

The only problem is that you don't realize it. So all that is required is letting go of thoughting, which requires no time at all. "Release is given you the instant you desire it."

So, "in any instant it is possible to have all this undone" and to realize your True Nature. "You do not have to seek reality. It will seek you and find you when you meet its conditions."

The only meditation technique required, then, is to open yourself up to its conditions, which essentially means detaching from compulsive thoughting.

When? Now! "[F]or *now* is the closest approximation of eternity that this world offers."

How? Detach from forms because you are bound to forms. A form is an object, which is anything singleoutable from other things, in other words, they are all the things we are able to perceive, imagine, or conceive. All thoughts are judgments, which are forms.

Here are three important tips.

First, stop trying to think your way out of dissatisfaction. "Adjustments of any kind are of the ego." It's the nature of the self you identify with that requires replacing. Nothing less will undermine dissatisfaction. Using meditation techniques to make little improvements won't suffice. Stop being satisfied with the secondary benefits and go after the primary benefits.

Second, if you think that you are on a spiritual journey, stop thinking that. All journeys require time. Living well requires no time.

Third, although it may seem counter-intuitive, pay much more attention to your body in the present moment. Rather, it's not really paying attention to the body as to the aliveness of the body. [I discuss this more in the next answer.] By focusing attention on physical sensations (such as breathing), you are automatically drawing attention away from thoughts.

The movement from (false) self to (true) Self is instantaneous.

There's nowhere to go, nothing to achieve, nothing to gain. You are already what you need to be to live well. "A journey from yourself does not exist . . .You cannot escape from what you are."

Realizing your true self is one way of talking about the goal of meditation techniques; the Zen way is to talk about realizing no-self. Either way it's discussed, realization take no time, whereas mastering meditation techniques requires time. This is why Shunryu Suzuki, Roshi, emphasized retaining beginner's mind.

On the other hand, doing meditation, which can only occur in the present moment, can foster detaching from forms. After all, since thoughts are very noisy and distracting, it helps to replace them with silence.

The still point is right here, right now – and you don't need any meditation techniques to find it.

Question: Is zen training necessary? Although I'd like spiritual improvement, I'm not interested in it at this time. What other options might help?

No, zen training is not required to overcome addiction to thinking. "Thoughting" is compulsive, unnecessary thinking that obstructs living well. All that is necessary is overcoming thoughting.

This sometimes happens spontaneously. You yourself have probably had moments of alert stillness uncontaminated by thoughts.

By using the words 'thinking' or 'thoughting' I am referring to conceptualizing. To understand is to conceptualize correctly. Concepts are principles of classification. We understand objects by classifying (sorting, dividing, discriminating, organizing, categorizing) them using concepts. For example, judging that this is a tree is grouping this object into a category with similar objects.

It's good to be able to think! We wouldn't be able to survive without sorting objects into groups like food, friend, dangerous, hot, and so on. There's nothing wrong with thinking.

However, having an addiction to thinking, always being attached to thinking, is a serious problem. For reasons I have tried to explain elsewhere, addiction to thinking is what creates dissatisfaction or suffering. **Dissatisfaction is optional** because freedom from thought addiction is possible.

Question: What are the different kinds of ways to eliminate suffering?

It can be very helpful to understand your options before selecting one. Actually, there are many, many different options. I have found **six** that I'd like to submit for your consideration. If one appeals to you more than the others, why not select it? Do what is required and see what happens.

Let's suppose that awareness (consciousness) is divisible into two domains: thinking (thought) and not-thinking (no-thought). Let's suppose that **living well requires living a balanced life** in the sense that it is necessary to spend considerable time both thinking and not-thinking. Let's further suppose that suffering is caused by spending almost no time not-thinking.

If so, **the cure is to find openings (portals, doors) from thinking to not-thinking and to go through those openings and spend time not-thinking.** It is only by doing that that you will be able to determine for yourself whether or not it is possible to free yourself from suffering. Again, it is not necessary to have an addiction to thinking. All sages are free from that.

First, **meditation** is, by far, the most popular opening to overcome addiction to thinking. It is the paradigmatic spiritual practice. The English word 'spiritual' comes from the Latin word designating breath or wind. Though there are many different kinds of meditation, what they have in common is that they all focus awareness on the natural physical process of breathing. It's a body practice.

So there's nothing necessarily religious or supernatural about meditation. More importantly, there's nothing conceptual about it either. The chief idea is to let go of thinking by paying full attention to your breathing.

(I provide step-by-step instructions for actually doing formal zen training in The Meditative Approach to Philosophy and in other books. A classic source is the much longer The Three Pillars of Zen by Roshi Philip Kapleau, who was the teacher of my teacher.)

The other five openings I'll mention here are much less discussed. If one of them interests you, I suggest both the written and audio works of Eckhart Tolle as an introduction. He discusses all five.

Second, **aliveness awareness** is another way to overcome addiction to thinking. It's an alternative to a meditation practice or it can be used as a supplement to a meditation practice. By 'aliveness awareness' I'm referring to paying attention to the sensations that come from the energy in your living body.

Obviously, your body is alive. It is not inert. Usually we are so busy thinking that we fail to notice how good it feels simply to be alive. Instead of focusing awareness on your breathing as in meditation (or your pulse), focus awareness on the tingling sensation that becomes noticeable in your hands when you lie quietly and still with your eyes closed. Then you may notice it in your feet, then up your legs and arms, and in your torso.

When you are paying full attention to the aliveness sensations of your body, you are not thinking. [I discuss this more below.]

Third, another way to overcome addiction to thinking is simply to pay full attention to your normal bodily **sensations** including such "inner" sensations as your posture and being upright. If you are, say, kneading dough or driving a car, pay full attention to the tactile sensations in your hands. Instead of kneading or steering automatically, devote all your attention to those perfectly ordinary sensations. If you do that, you will not be thinking; instead, you'll be fully aware of them without thinking anything.

Fourth, yet another way to overcome addiction to thinking is to practice saying **"yes" to the present moment** regardless of what is unfolding. Allow the present moment to be just as it is. Why not? It already is just as it is anyway. If you try to resist reality, reality always wins. Why fight when you have a zero chance of winning the fight?

This can be even stronger than merely accepting or allowing the present moment to be as it is. It helps to pretend that you yourself have actually chosen it. This seems crazy when you are suffering, but, if you try it, you may experience for yourself how it helps.

It's a bit like this: suppose that your beloved cheated on you with someone else. Imagining them having sex makes you nauseous. However, if you are able to make yourself imagine them having sex, even just that level of acceptance may be able to reduce your suffering. Why? It's a way of practicing not taking it personally.

By saying "yes" to the present moment and allowing what-is to be just as it (already) is, you are practicing not taking it personally. This can initially seem bizarre, but, if you practice it, I predict that you'll find that it works.

Fifth, another way to overcome an addiction to thinking is **deciding to stop thinking** and just stopping. There's nothing except your own habit of incessantly thinking that is causing you to think incessantly. Some people, so I've heard, are able to stop thinking by simply deciding to do so.

Like aliveness awareness, this, too, can be combined with meditation. For example, if you are meditating and find yourself telling yourself a story to occupy your mind, you may be able simply to decide to stop telling stories and, instead, to focus wholeheartedly on your breathing.

Sixth, **cravings** are also openings to not-thinking. They can be used to overcome addiction to thinking. If you are a smoker who craves a cigarette, suddenly you may find yourself smoking without even being aware of obtaining and lighting the cigarette. The first step in becoming a nonsmoker is simply to become aware of what you are doing. Instead of automatically smoking whenever you have a craving, simply notice the craving.

This goes for any kind of craving. Before you do anything, simply notice the craving. You may or may not decide to satisfy it–that is secondary. What is of primary importance is simply to pay full attention to the craving itself. What happens to it if you don't instantly smoke (or eat or have sex or have a drink)?

Find out. It may simply vanish. It may become stronger. The point is to put awareness in front of the behavior.

This especially applies to emotional impulses, which are cravings If I slap you in the face and you find yourself angry and inclined to respond in kind, before you respond, stop! Become aware. You do not have to slap me back. You feel like slapping me back, but it is not necessary actually to do so. Why let impulses govern your life? You may or may not decide to slap me back, but wouldn't you be wise not to do it automatically?

So there are **six openings to not-thinking**. You have plenty of options. If you are not already using one of these every day, I encourage you to begin to do so. As you notice your dissatisfactions diminish, you'll be glad that you did.

Permit me to be more detailed about dropping thoughts in favor of awareness of your life energy. When you directly focus on your life energy, you are automatically detaching from thoughts.

It's possible to practice focusing on your life energy.

The possibility of doing so was realized thousands of years ago. It's described in many Buddhist sutras. There are meditative practices about doing an "inner" body scan. It's recently been popularized by such teachers as Thich Nhat Hanh and Eckhart Tolle.

Isn't there far too much concern about the external form and appearance of our bodies?

After all, physical objects are ultimately shimmering clumps of energy. Anyone who has ever cared for a house or an automobile realizes that they deteriorate as time goes by; they never stay the same. All of us are aging and, so, we are sometimes very aware that our bodies are in incessant flux.

It's extremely useful to let go of thinking (conceptualizing, thoughting) about our bodies. It's extremely useful to bypass our intellects and directly experience them.

Why?

By doing so you are freeing yourself from identification with your body. Yes, of course, you are your body, but you are much more than your body. To get stuck only identifying with your body eliminates the possibility of identifying with more than your body.

In fact, practicing the following exercise regularly to become aware of your aliveness may also benefit your body by strengthening its ability to heal itself.

Here's one way to do it. Become physically still in a quiet place. For example, lie flat on your back with your hands resting comfortably on the tops of your hips. Close your eyes.

Become aware of the life energy in your hands.
Do not think about the life energy in your hands. Do not ask your intellect if there is life energy in your hands. Let go of thinking and just focus on the life energy that is in your hands.

Don't worry: it's there. Just notice it. Simply become aware of it. Hold your attention there.

You may notice a slight tingling in them. As you practice the exercise more and more, you may notice a sensation of energy or aliveness. (As usual, language doesn't work well in such matters.)

Practice this every day for a few days. Soon you may not even have to close your eyes or be still to feel it.
Then extend your focus in sequence to various other parts of your body such as your feet, legs, arms, stomach, chest, and so on. Eventually, you'll be able to experience directly the aliveness throughout your body.

Make this exercise into a habit. It's not only a way of feeling more alive in the present moment, it's a way of getting beyond the prison of conceptual thinking.

Please help yourself. There is plenty of peace of mind for everyone. You'll be glad that you did.

First, it is very simple.

Second, it is quickly mastered in the sense that it takes very little time to learn to get really good at it.

Third, is can be effective.

The problem with any traditional spiritual or meditative practice or technique is that it requires time to master. This fosters the idea that spiritual mastery is a goal to be attained at some future time.

There's something seriously wrong about that. The Buddha himself repeatedly says that, although it requires striving, awakening can happen quickly — even, theoretically, in just a day.

All goals are to be achieved in the future. Anything involving the future inherently involves thinking. Where, outside thought, is the future? The future has no reality outside thinking. **Thinking obstructs realization**, which can only occur in the present moment.

Like all awareness (consciousness), aliveness awareness is right here right now. The idea is simply to focus on sensing parts of the body from within, which automatically draws attention away from thoughts.

My experience is that aliveness awareness works well with zazen. There's little difference between feeling the breath infuse itself throughout the body and feeling the aliveness inside the body.

It's true that aliveness awareness requires you to pay attention to, for example, the sensations inside your hands (and feet and legs and arms and so on). You may be so attached to thoughts that, initially, that is difficult. If so, just stick with it. Just do aliveness awareness for a few minutes every day. You'll soon (in a few days or a week or so) begin to feel it.

Don't worry: your life energy is there. Your cells, too, are alive. It's just that you are so lost in thought that you don't notice their aliveness. Life energy training corrects that.

Again, it's simple, easy, and effective. It doesn't require any special equipment or training. It can be done for just 5 or 10 or 15 minutes. Why not do just three 10-minute sessions daily, one in the morning, one in the afternoon, and one in the evening?

If you aren't doing any practice at all to weaken thoughting, I'll bet that you notice that that one is working for you after only a week or two.

If you already have a practice and are looking for a boost, I also recommend life energy training.

Permit me to give the Buddha the last words [from Anguttara Nikaya 7:70; IV 139; Bhikkhu Bodhi, tr.]: "Meditate," he says, "do not be negligent, or else you will regret it later."

Question: What is body practice? What does it have to do with wisdom?

Though they do it in different ways, sages not infrequently talk about body practice. What are they talking about? Is it important?

If you are one of the many people who are confused about the nature of a spiritual practice, the answers will surprise you.

For example, many people think of Buddhism as a religion. Buddhists, on this view, are different from other people because they accept a distinctive creed or set of beliefs.

No, to be a Buddhist is to practice Buddhism. Except for the belief that doing so might be helpful, it is not necessary to believe anything to practice Buddhism.

Another way to say this is that being a Buddhist involves practicing physically. Another way to say *this* is that being a Buddhist means regularly doing a body practice.

No body practice, no buddhism. That explains why sages often talk about body practice (though they don't always use those words).

Being wise is not thinking in a certain way. <u>It's false that wisdom is a set of thoughts or beliefs.</u> **Wisdom is practiced.**

John Daido Loori: "Taking responsibility for our life includes taking responsibility for our body . . . Body practice means realizing the Way with the body as well as with the mind."

A concrete example may help. This example is a real one that's based on the fact that it's often easier to notice a flaw in someone else than it is to notice it in ourselves.

Years back into the last century I had a girlfriend who would visit me. She would often stride down the hall obviously focused so intently on where she was going that she would bang her heels on the floor. It was impossible not to notice: the cottage where I lived at that time was small and had only one hall. That was not the controlled, mindful tread of a sage.

I knew that she was very unhappy and spent a lot of time thinking about how to distract herself so she'd enjoy life more. The problem wasn't that I felt superior to her. The problem was that I identified with her unhappiness.

She walked that way because her goal-focused thoughts were separated from her body, her walking. Since separation is the cause of dissatisfaction, it was obvious just from how she was walking that she was hurting. Instead of being her walking, her mind was focused only on where she was going, which means that it was separated from what she was doing because she was thinking about some future event.

How do you walk? Don't you, too, often walk lost in thought?

Here's the alternative: walk well. Each step can be a body practice, a mini-meditation. Each step is a mini-meditation only if it is taken with awareness. Whether you arrive where you are headed or not, you won't miss the present moment if you pay attention to what you are doing and live mindfully.

As you may understand, there is walking meditation as well as sitting meditation.

As Thich Nhat Hanh writes in Being Peace, and this you may not understand, "The sitting and the walking must be extended to the non-walking, non-sitting moments of our day. That is the basic principle of meditation."

The word 'practice' in the phrase 'body practice' is misleading. It's not really the best word, though similar words like 'training' aren't any better. Usually we think of practicing in order to do better in the future. The point of meditation, however, is to do better right now. After all, the present moment is the only moment we ever get to live.

The method of meditation is to focus on whatever we are doing right now. Each act becomes a mini-meditation. This avoids doing one thing while thinking about another.

Another way to talk about body practice is to talk about separating thinking from awareness (or Becoming from Being). As long as we stay trapped in thinking (time, Becoming), we will seek the purpose or meaning of life elsewhere in time, usually, in the future.

Freeing ourselves from thinking (time, Becoming) is negating time. Once time is negated, the only place to find the purpose or meaning of life is in the present moment, in whatever we are doing right now.

Turning this around, finding the purpose or meaning of life in the present moment is negating thinking (time, Becoming). As Eckhart Tolle writes in A New Earth: "When you look upon what you do or where you are as the main purpose of your life, you negate time."

So, for example, walking down a hall can be excellent body practice. The meaning of your life when you are walking down a hall is to be walking down that hall. The purpose of the walking is to get somewhere else, but that purpose is secondary.

To have an effective body practice is to treat everything you do as if it were intrinsically valuable and worthwhile instead of treating everything you do merely as a means to some other end.

The value and fullness of life are available here and now.

Where else could they be available? The past is a set of thoughts that, at best, are accurate rememberings, and the future is nothing but a set of thoughts that are mere imaginings.

The value of life does not come from thinking about it.

The value of life comes from life itself.

This is <u>very good news:</u> making each act a body practice is not only simple enough that everyone can do it, but it's the only way really to enjoy life.

Question: Is there a quick fix for refocusing on the present moment?

A spiritual practice is a breathing practice. It doesn't have to last a long time to be effective. Here's a simple breathing practice that came from India and has recently been popularized by Andy Weil. It only takes about 90 seconds (for 4 cycles), and it should be practiced at least twice daily.

You'll find it a relaxing tonic. If you already have another spiritual practice like zazen, you may use this as a warm-up.

Exhale.

Place the tip of your tongue touching the inside of the ridge that is just above the inner surface of your front teeth and leave it there throughout this breathing practice. With your lips and teeth closed, inhale through your nose for a silent count of 4.

Hold your breath for a silent count of 7.

With your lips and teeth open, exhale completely for a count of 8 while making an audible "whoosing" sound.

Repeat this cycle at least 4 times and resume breathing normally.

If you practice this in public, modify step 5 so that you are exhaling silently.

What's important is the 4/7/8 ratio—not how long your counts are.

I suggest always using the practice upon arising in the morning and just before going to sleep at night. Also, please use it whenever you feel yourself beginning to get upset or agitated for any reason. If you are especially upset, just increase the cycles from 4 up to 8. You are not limited to doing it only twice daily.

It can be done sitting, lying, or standing.

It really is relaxing and very easy to do. It may seem so simple that it couldn't possibly help, but please just do it twice daily for several weeks so that you master it. That's the only trick to it. Surely you have 3 minutes daily to begin to quiet the mind.

You'll be glad that you did.

Question: I've heard of "mini-meditation." That may be something that I can do. What is it? Is it easier? How do you do it?

Frequently using mini-meditation is an effective way to bring Being into Becoming, to realize your True Self.

You may want awakening but fear that you lack the will power for extended periods of formal meditation. The reality may surprise you: though some humans have more than others, nobody is blessed with a lot of will-power. So please don't ever beat yourself up because you don't have much of it.

Instead, work with reality to live better. With respect to will-power, this means making the best use of a small amount.

How?

By establishing automatic behaviors, habits, that are effective in promoting what is valuable. A good example, which I've discussed previously, is establishing an effective morning ritual [see the next answer].

Another is using mini-meditation. What is it? Why use it frequently?

A mini-meditation is nothing but a short meditation: it's simply **being conscious of breathing for one or two or three breaths.**

That's it. It's that easy. It's that simple.

Since a meditation is a waking up from the incessant stream of thoughting or thought forms that plague us, a mini-meditation is like a brief glance towards no-thought (freedom from thoughting) that can be as bracing as a splash of cold water on your face in the morning.

Since breath is formless, paying attention to it – even briefly – weakens identification with such forms as thoughts, bodily sensations, and emotions.

There's nothing you have to do except **pay attention**. That's all that is required to realize Being, to open to the formless, to bring Being into Becoming, to awaken to your True Nature.

Establishing a mini-meditation practice is establishing the habit of remembering to let go of forms frequently throughout the day.

The best way to do this is to **link routine behaviors with mini-meditation.** Here are some examples. If these don't resonate with you, just use other ones that are similar. Do a mini-meditation each time you:

- Brush or floss your teeth
- Put on shoes or boots
- Open a car door and get in
- Pour liquid into a glass, mug, or cup
- Raise a glass, mug, or cup to your mouth to drink
- Look at the moon for the first time in an evening
- Shiver
- Hear a telephone ring and begin to pick it up
- Stop at a stop sign or traffic light
- Enter your workplace
- Hug someone
- Enter your home

Those are sufficient to give you the idea. Even if you just added one every few weeks, in a few months you'd soon be much more present in your own life. Monks and nuns often memorize gathas to repeat silently to themselves as they do various repetitive acts to help them focus on the present moment instead of being lost thoughting.

How could you enjoy life without being aware of it?

Here's the important fact behind this recommendation to use mini-meditation frequently: sages are always meditating.

You may have the false belief that sages only meditate during periods of formal meditation such as when they are still and seated on meditation cushions. No, the idea behind such formal mediation is not to emulate tree stumps.

Formal stilling meditation can be useful for fostering stillness of mind. A still mind is fully alert, awake, and conscious, but empty of thoughts. It's impossible to think while simultaneously focusing on the formless. Even in formal meditation, it's impossible to be aware of more than one thought at a time.

To live well is to live much or most of the time with a still mind.

We are all creatures of habit. We tend to think the same kinds of thoughts, to eat the same kinds of foods, to talk with the same kinds of people, and so on.

So the issue is not whether or not to have habits. The only issue is whether or not to have habits that are effective in promoting what is valuable.

Linking routine daily doings with breath consciousness fosters spiritual awakening. Since a still mind is free from attending to forms, it is open to Being. Since our human purpose is to be as open to Being as possible, the habit of frequently being aware of breathing is a valuable one.

You'll have more periods during the day when you are untroubled by forms. The more such periods you have, the more you will enjoy life and the more you will emulate sages.

Life is lived in the present moment. It is impossible to live in the past or future.

It is impossible to live life in the past or in the future, because the one no longer exists and the other does not yet exist. Past and future are nothing but thoughts.

They are sets of thought forms. The only reality they have depends upon our thinking *now* about them.

All problems exist in the past or in the future; **problems require time.**

Being is timeless. Now is the only possible opening to Being.

Therefore, the more you open to Being, the less troubled you will be by problems. Practicing this way really is a very clever way to enjoy life.

Developing the habit of mini-meditations is an effective way to open to Being and, so, live better.

Question: How can I learn without books and without a teacher?

I don't know. Here, though, are two suggestions. They both involve paying more attention to your environment and less attention to thoughts.

First, pay greater attention to nonhuman animals. What do they have to teach us?

Albert Einstein: "Look deep into nature, and then you will understand everything better."

Why did he think that? How might that work?

I think it's chiefly because, as David Abram argues in his excellent book The Spell of the Sensuous , we are unhappy primarily because we are locked in our literate intellects. For all its benefits, with literacy comes a natural fall into incessant thinking about the human-made world. Paying greater attention to animals can help us to notice and correct that fall from grace.

Most humans live in ways that suggest that they believe that we have little or nothing of value to learn from animals. I not only disagree with that belief, but I think there is an extraordinarily valuable lesson that we can learn from animals about how to be happier.

I was taught it again late one recent morning. As is my habit, while gazing towards the lake I was sipping tea before a "round" of zazen. There happened to be a heron fishing right in front of my cottage. I delayed my meditation to watch the heron. After about 15 minutes, it ceased fishing and flew off–presumably to try to find a better spot.

What was it doing? Fishing. **What else was it doing? Nothing.**

That's the lesson: **wholeheartedly do whatever you are doing.** Specifically, do not think about anything else while doing it.

In my office I keep a framed photograph of a polar bear lying on the ice on its belly intently watching a seal's breathing hole. That polar bear is living well.

Have you ever watched a completely still cat outside a mouse's hole alert for the appearance of the mouse?

I heard a story of a Sufi master who, when asked how he became spiritually awake, said it was simply by watching how cats live and emulating them.

Imagine that you are a frog on a lily pad waiting for a suitable insect to land within reach of your tongue. Also imagine that you have a broken leg. Since you are still, let's imagine that there is no pain in your leg (although there will be the next time you move it). Here's the key question: *would you be dissatisfied?*

Not if you were a frog.

However, if you were a human in a frog's body, you would probably be asking questions such as: Why me? Why did I have to break my leg? How can I be expected to do what I have to do with a broken leg? Why can't I be resting in bed rather than out trying to feed myself? Why can't I just be enjoying life like other frogs? Why do these things always happen to me?

The alert stillness practiced by herons, polar bears, cats, and frogs is incompatible with suffering. While some pain is normally inevitable, dissatisfaction is optional. **No unnecessary thought, no dissatisfaction.**

We humans have the distinctive and useful ability to think, to conceptualize. Especially after we have acquired literacy to solidify our thoughts, we unintentionally become bound in our human-made surrealities. In effect, we get lost in a maze of distinctions and lose sight of the unity of the whole. Until we find our way again, we remain stuck, unhappy, hurting. Dissatisfaction is the price we pay for thinking too much.

Humans are the only dissatisfied animals. No other kinds of animals are unhappy.

The primary, perhaps sole, reason for that is that no other kinds of animals get stuck living in their thoughts. I don't mean that they are not conscious; I simply mean that their thoughts (judgements, conceptualizations), if they make them, don't frequently dominate their lives. By way of contrast, we must notice and then strive to stop unnecessary thoughts if we are ever to experience stillness and genuine peace.

If so, we can learn from animals the way out. Emulate them. When doing something, just do it. While you are doing it, don't be thinking about something else. Focus. Pay attention. Pay full attention.

How can we learn to live like that? The same way we learn other skills: practice. Practice focusing every day. Be persistent. If you do it well, your excess thoughts will more and more tend to become absorbed into your activities. More and more you'll forget your self (ego) with all its incessant worries and concerns, restlessness, and fears.

In other words, learn from animals how to let go of all unnecessary distinctions such as the self/other distinction. One way out of the trap of incessant thinking, the way to break the compulsion always to be conceptualizing, really is to look deeply at the natural world. What animals do naturally, we–with our literate intellects–have to teach ourselves to do. The more you practice **alert stillness (no-thought, Presence)**, the happier you will be.

Don't take it from me; I'm not a sage; instead, learn from animals.

This is at least part of the explanation about why so many humans are passionate about animals. For example, people often become very attached to their pets. One reason for this is that, for many people, the only regular access to no-thought they have is indirectly through their pets.

Second, and Eckhart Tolle is terrific at encouraging this, notice yourself noticing beauty. Witnessing that awareness can be liberating. Permit me to suggest a few examples and then draw your attention to an important commonality among them.

Nature is full of stunning spectacles. Doesn't everyone understand that there is nothing more mentally refreshing than breaking beyond the bounds of our human world?

Have you spent any time at all paying attention to the beauty of recent sunrises or sunsets? (If not, why not?) The magnificent scenery in mountain ranges is stunning. Remember, too, noticing beauty in stark deserts.

I have always loved watching the wind play in the leaves of trees, and I'm fortunate to have a cottonwood tree in front of my home next to the lakeshore. I can, and do, spend hours watching that spectacle.

Have you ever become absorbed just watching what a breeze does to blades of grass? Lie down on your belly and have a good look.

Most months of the year, I am treated to the beauty of diamonds dancing each sunny morning on the surface of a lake. When the lake is frozen and snow covered, the reflected light often has its own kind of dazzling beauty.

Are you open to noticing beauty in unusual places? Just try to imagine, for example, all the beauty that was missed by all humans — less lucky than we — who lived before the age of microscopes and telescopes.

Though we often rush past them, it's difficult to miss the beauty of finished wood in furniture or cabinets or the beautiful shapes of interesting buildings.

What about favorite melodies from your favorite composers?

Aren't we all captivated by beautiful human forms? Whether in sculptures or in the flesh, don't we tend to stare with thoughtless amazement?

I recall with a smile how I had to learn as a teenager to protect myself from beautiful female forms. Females are typically at their peak of physical beauty around the age of 16 (according to the Buddha) or 18 (according to me). I'm not here referring to lust. I'm talking about protecting myself from thoughtless idiocy.

After all, when I was that age myself, on school days I had to interact with many such fair specimens. Simply gaping in silent awe would have given away too much power. I learned, and so did at least some of my peers, how to find some flaw or other as a point to steady and reclaim our identities. There was always something — less than beautiful toes or knees, perhaps, or too thin upper arms, or even just a less than wholly pleasing voice. I felt it important not to get too sucked in.

Poets and other artists, of course, know all about noticing beauty.

If I've helped you to recall your own experiences noticing beauty, please ask: "What do they all have in common?"

Noticing beauty always involves alert, thoughtless awareness.

That is what, as a teenager, I thought I had to protect myself from. I was temporarily unable to sustain my own identity even when confronted momentarily by beauty.

Fool!

The identity that I was protecting was only one that I had created from my own thoughts. It was, in other words, my ego or self, the story or narrative that separates me from everyone else. That's nothing like my real identity.

Like yours, my real identity is beyond thought. Awareness of Being requires no-thought. Stopping thinking, even for just a moment, is sufficient to experience no-thought, direct and unmediated awareness of what-is. Instead of resisting those experiences of alert, thoughtless awareness, I wish I had been more open to them. Yes, of course, my thoughts are part of me, but they are, I realize now, only a very small part compared to the vast spaciousness beyond thought.

Noticing beauty is an opening to no-thought. No-thought is the approach to Being.

Please, be open to it. Whenever you notice yourself noticing beauty, *allow* that experience rather than resisting it like a foolish teenager.

Who you are is beautiful. Instead of being separate from beauty itself, you are part of it. That itself is a stunning realization.

When you allow beauty to suspend thinking, even for a moment, that is realizing your True-Self (Buddha-Nature).

Please test for yourself whether or not Emerson's claim that "beauty is never quite absent from our eyes" is true.

Wouldn't you like to live wisely (live well, live as a sage)?

Practice allowing no-thought as experience; practice not allowing thought to mediate experience.

You don't have to do, gain, or accomplish anything. It's simply a matter of dropping all your defenses, letting go of all useless thoughts. Though it's not easy, it's simple.

It's ironic: instead of protecting yourself, all you are doing is preventing yourself from realizing your true nature. Sometimes Nature's cataclysmic events are so awe-inspiriting that it's impossible to avoid experiencing no-thought momentarily. Nature's beauty, though, is all around us, but it's often obscured by thought. One of the functions of art is to get us to experience it, to see what-is by looking freshly, to lift us out of our comfortable conceptual ruts. This is at least part of the explanation about why many humans are so passionate about art.

Question: Can journal writing help reduce thoughts?

Whether or not you are trained as an artist, you may sometimes wonder about becoming more creative.
I believe that we are all naturally creative and that our only serious problem with creativity is uncovering it. Given that we are naturally creative, it may seem odd to think

about creativity training. The difficulty comes because **we unintentionally block our own creativity.**

The chief way that we retard our own creativity is by thinking too much. Instead of relaxing and letting our instincts (brain) respond appropriately to novel circumstances, we get stuck in our thoughts.

The best kind of creativity training is mastering a body or breathing (spiritual) practice such as zazen meditation. There is nothing better at vacating, emptying, the mind, nothing better at getting unstuck. Any practice is valuable if it results in no-thought.

I've discovered another kind of creativity training, namely, "**morning pages**," if you wish to supplement or replace a breathing practice. Like zazen meditation, it's very simple.

Unlike zazen meditation, it is also easy and of limited duration. The catch, however, is that you must do it each morning, without fail, for ninety days. If you are unwilling to do that with no excuses, don't bother with morning pages at all.

I learned about morning pages from The Artist's Way by Julia Cameron with Mark Bryan. She claims it is "the primary tool of creative recovery." Again, we are all naturally creative. Why not assume that you are, too?

Actually, we must be or we would be unable to solve the problems presented by the ceaseless flux in which we live. So the task of creativity training is simply to uncover what is already there.

Here is the practice of morning pages: **write three pages, single-spaced, of longhand writing each morning when you arise that is strictly steam of consciousness.** That's it.

You may use a spiral notebook or a loose-leaf binder. The pages should be standard size, namely, 8 1/2 by 11 inches, with narrow (college ruled) lines. As soon as you write your three pages each morning, put them away for at least a couple of months, in other words, do not look at them for at least sixty days.

Do not show them to anyone else. (If you know you are going to do that, you will censor your writing, which will prevent it from being stream of consciousness.)

Fill three whole pages without fail each morning for a minimum of three months.

You may write about anything at all. Much of what you write may be negative or petty or inconsequential. Feel free to be whiny, bitter, or even angry. Feel free to be hopeful. It is even alright to be delusional! **Any topic is acceptable.** You can always write about your friends or relatives, or, even the weather.

It may not be easy at first, but it will become easier with daily practice. Just make yourself do it. The more difficult you find it initially, the more it may unblock you. Those who find it a difficult habit to establish often benefit the most from establishing it. Believe it or not, you may unleash so much valuable creativity that you may decide to do morning pages every morning for the rest of your life.

Morning pages work to nurture creativity because they are an effective way of freeing yourself from the tyranny of your own thoughts. Writing your thoughts down enables you to get rid of them. This is especially true if you have, like most people, an inner perfectionist censor who is always belittling or mocking you. That censor's statements are false, and writing them down enables you to free yourself from them.

You should be skeptical or questioning about morning pages (and everything else I've written in this book). That's good. Please do not, however, be stuck on negativity. Test all the ideas for yourself.

How good would you feel if you force yourself to use a simple daily tactic for three months and it turns out to unleash an enormous amount of your spontaneous originality? Try it. You'll discover that it is excellent creativity training, and you'll be very pleased that you tried it.

This tactic is so effective that it is sometimes even recommended by meditation teachers. The idea is to keep a pad and pencil next to your meditation cushion and, when you get stuck in some thought train, jot it down and resume meditating. You might want to try it.

On the other hand, I myself don't recommend it. It's better to teach yourself how to let the thought train go without moving by dropping it and returning your focus to the practice.

After all, when you are writing down thoughts, you are thinking.

It reminds me of the story about a novelist. He kept a pad and pencil next to his bed so that, on occasions when he woke up dreaming, he could jot down the content of his dreams to provide fresh material for his stories.

One morning when he was brushing his teeth, he remembered that he had awakened during the night and written down an important story line from a dream he'd been having. He rushed back to his bedroom to find out what he had written. The note simply read, "boy meets girl."

About the Author

I was born 3 July 1946 in Teaneck, New Jersey, U.S.A. I grew up in Toledo, Ohio, where I attended Deveaux elementary school and, from grades 5 through 11, the schools in Ottawa Hills. I graduated from Blair Academy in 1964. I was a pre-professional philosophy major at Syracuse University and graduated in 1968. After two years as an Army lieutenant with overseas duty in Korea from 1969-1971, I attended graduate school at The University of Iowa where I received an M.A. (1974) and Ph.D. (1977).

I taught humanities and philosophy at SUNY Geneseo from 1977 to 2009. Some of the over 20 books I've written are listed near the beginning of this book. I founded the Ironox Works, Inc., publishing company in 2004; cf. ironoxworks.com. I am co-author of http://www.lasting-weight-loss.com/

I'm a former member of MENSA and the American Philosophical Association. I played hockey for many years in the Rochester Metro Hockey League. I've been a member of the Rochester Zen Center for twenty years. I taught many undergraduates how to "sit" and lead a meditation group each week at a local prison. I live happily alone on the shore of Conesus Lake, which is the westernmost of the Finger Lakes in upstate New York.

For more about me, visit the Amazon Author Central page at: http://www.amazon.com/-/e/B0047EI11A

If you'd like to connect with me on social media, just go to: http://www.linkedin.com/pub/dennis-e-bradford/1a/a2a/524/ You'll also find there how easy it is to contact me should you wish to do so. Also, http://www.facebook.com/dennis.bradford.313 as well as http://www.twitter.com/dennisebradford

I encourage you to visit my blog on wisdom and well-being: http://dennis-bradford.com . Its posts are grouped in terms of six kinds of well-being (in no particular order) on the sidebar, namely, financial, moral (inter-personal), intellectual, physical, emotional, and spiritual. I encourage you to begin with whatever interests you most. Please feel free to leave comments. I happen to think that there's an enormous amount of free, valuable content there.

If you are interested in finding out more about my other books, they are available in various places, including: http://www.amazon.com. (Simply select 'Books' or 'Kindle store' and do a search for 'Dennis E Bradford').

I've a **favor** to ask. While you are at amazon.com, will you please find this book and leave some feedback about it? Please let others benefit from your judgment. It will surely help them and possibly help me. Thank you in advance.

May you realize your True Nature.

Best Suggestions for More Help

There are posts in the spiritual well-being category of my blog that may interest you. Go to: http://dennis-bradford.com.

For more on zen training as a way of mastering life, see my Mastery in 7 Steps.

The books and trainings of Eckhart Tolle are excellent.

For reading more about zen training and Buddhist practice, the best book is still Roshi Kapleau's The Three Pillars of Zen (2nd ed.). There are plenty of other good books about zen training as well. You can find a list of them, including some excellent collections of Buddhist sutras, in the top three categories under the RECOMMENDED READING tab at the top of the home page of my freefromdennis.com website.

Here's the rule:

If reading helps you to practice, read; if reading distracts you from practicing, don't read. What goes for reading goes for everything else, too.

Wake up!